Ultimate Traeger Grill & Smoker Cookbook

*The Complete Wood Pellet Smoker And Grill
Manual. Tasty Recipes For The Perfect Bbq*

Steven Devon

Table of Contents

Introduction

The Traeger grill is one of the most sold products in the market today. While most people know about this product, others have never heard about it before. Here, we would give you enough information about the Traeger grill so you can understand enough about it and whether it can be useful for you, your home, and your business. At the end of everything, you would love the Traeger grill over the charcoal and gas grill.

Traeger grills are outdoor cookers that utilize modern technologies to ignite all- natural hard traegers as a fuel source for heating and cooking your food. They are an electric-powered, automated device for precisely cooking your food with a delicious wood-fired taste.

When using a Traeger grill, you can take great pride in the fact that you are cooking your food with a cleaner-burning fuel source, which is safe and efficient. Using this type of grill you will not have to worry about the strong, harsh smells from heavy smoke and gases that come from using a traditional charcoal or propane grill.

A great outdoor cooking experience does not have to be complicated. It should be easy and relaxing. A Traeger grill can provide this relaxing environment and give you many years of highly enjoyable cooking experiences.

If you live in a small or medium area, where you have limited backyard space use, and do not want to spend the extra money on a charcoal grate, the Traeger is the perfect option for you. When you grill using this product, you are sure to have everything in your grill in place for you to have a good time while grilling food. This product is perfect for grilling fish, meat, kabobs, steaks, chicken, and more.

How much does it cost?

This product is quite affordable and effective. You will be able to use this for a long time without having to worry about rusting or breaking. The best thing about this grill is that it generally costs less than $500 and it lasts for a long time.

On the other hand, the Traeger is a grill that will give you the following benefits when using it:

- You can easily smoke your food if you have the right fuel.
- The Traeger grill is a portable grill that you can carry around with you on most occasions.
- This product makes cooking a lot easier as you need to assemble the grill with the right fuel.
- The gas that comes out of each Traeger grill is clean and does not destroy the flavor of your cooking ingredients.

The benefits of using the Traeger grill are clearly evident and you will notice what you are missing by not using it. However, you need to check out the price of this product to make sure you are getting quality services.

Shopping Guide

How Do Traeger Smokers Work?

Once you plug in the grill and adjust the fire to a remote system, the traegers are moved and transformed into fire and smoke. One of the most essential aspects of a traeger smoker is the unit. The machine controls the temperature in your traeger cooker all over the pot.

There are some common kinds of grill controllers:

- Three-position controls: Generally found on cheaper traeger cookers, these controls are set to three configurations, low (225 °F) medium (325 °F), and high (425 °F). We are often referred to as LMH controls. During set intervals, they feed the traegers into the furnace, and you do not have a large amount of temperature power.
- Multi-position controllers: These controls can be used in smaller increments to adjust the temperature. Traegers are fed in set loops that also do not give great precision to these controllers. In optimal settings, a multi-position controller is normally accurate + /- 20 °F. The inclusion of a Led panel is a good function of these devices.
- Non-PID device with one-touch: This form of control helps you to change the temperature in increments of 5–10 °F. In fixed cycles, they still feed traegers, which means that they can solely deliver + /- 15–20 °F accuracy. They also have LCD screens, one-touch controls, and many have meat sample inputs.
- PID controllers: Many found PID controllers to be the gold norm for grill controls. Temperatures are only a few degrees

correct. Such a device method will also handle a programmable meat sample that operates in conjunction with the control mechanism to reduce the temperature until the meat is done. The traeger feed is constantly controlled to maintain the right temperature. They do have one-touch buttons and an LCD.

Durability and Construction Material

Don't be misled by an enticing traeger grill exterior. The maker may have made costs and used inexpensive parts to pick up on the interior even though there is plenty of stainless steel on the outside.

If you are looking at a BBQ built from stainless steel, make sure it has a really good quality coating. As long as the paint blisters and chips continue to rust, the cooker deteriorates.

It can also be remembered that a traeger smoker made of high-quality materials is safer. High-quality materials preserve heat, allow a more effective use of traegers, and help sustain the temperature during cold weather.

Size of the Hopper

Your traeger cooker's hopper is the tub that houses the traegers ready to go into the furnace. The scale of your hopper thus ultimately determines the length of your cooks. Therefore, it proves irritating to settle for a hopper that's too low, as your cooks won't be distant.

As a guide, you will find a traeger grill with a 40-pound hopper at the standard smoking temperatures for about 40 hours. In view of the fact that some cooks take about 20 hours, for example, an 18-pound hopper will be problematic.

And remember, your cooker will use even more fuel to raise the smoker and maintain temperature when you live in a colder climate.

You can buy hopper extensions for your grill traeger. Make sure that the hopper extender you are purchasing is compatible with your traeger smoker and the supplier is healthy.

Plan How Much Cooking Real Estate You Need

You have to ask yourself a few questions before you know how big your cooker needs to be. How many people am I going to cook for? Do I plan to cook huge cuts or even a whole pig?

An unusual characteristic of traeger smokers is that the cooking region is also dry. As a rule, there should be no variation in temperature between the top rack and the bottom rack during cooking.

Despite this, let us think about the disparity between the primary cooking area and the total cooking region. The central cooking field applies to the field on the central pot. The overall cooking area takes secondary racks into account.

A broad cooker with a primary cooking area of 500 square inches may therefore be of less benefit to you than a cooker with a limited cooking area which includes a primary 450 square inch rack and a secondary 125 square inch rack. When you cannot be bothered to do arithmetic, 575 square centimeters of the total area for cooking.

The bottom line is—make an inventory of what you need and don't presume that it's cheaper.

Common features and Capabilities

In comparison to the typical charcoal or offset smokers, a whole lot of bells and whistles may be used with traeger grills. Some of the features you should consider include:

- WIFI: companies are beginning to benefit from the fact that traeger smokers have a designed computer inside them. By integrating Wi-Fi, the temperature of your grill can be monitored and controlled from almost anywhere, as long as there is an internet connection. Companies such as Green Mountain Grills also provide free software that you can access and use for supreme convenience.

- Meat samples: Some traeger cookers have controlled outputs to allow meat samples to be plugged in directly. You can then see readings taken from your meat easily on your cooker's computer.

- Grilling options: Traeger cookers have a downside in the past because of their lack of grilling capabilities. Some manufacturers have made it possible to grill either by removing part of the diffuser plate or by supplying a special grilling area in the cooker.

- Add-ons: Manufacturers often offer a range of supplements. Check for the standard features and what add-ons are at a surcharge. Some add-ons are offered independently from the manufacturer by companies. If your particular cooker has an essential feature but is not a standard feature, make sure it is available as an add-on before you buy the cooker.

Length of Warranty

In traeger smokers there are some relatively high-tech components. Moving parts are also available, such as the hammer. This means that your cooker may break down and you may not be able to fix it. Make sure you understand exactly how your warranty is extended, what it will cover, what it is void, and where your smoker will need to get in for any reparations.

Traeger Consumption

No one loves a traeger dog, a traeger burner that chews needless traegers.

If your traeger cooker is too thin, the cooker's body loses heat. It uses a lot of traegers to keep the temperature.

You will also use many traegers if the metal is too thick. The walls of a thick smoker act as a 'heat sink.' Heat is removed from the stove and stored in the cooker's walls. So, it takes a lot of traegers to reach the desired temperature in the cooking area. Although thick walls are desirable for certain types of cookers, in traeger smokers they are not required.

Research and discover how many traegers the smoker burn per hour. Everything up to one pound an hour is OK at smoking temperatures. Bruce Bjorkman of MAK, for example, claims that his barbecues only use about ½ pound an hour for the smoke.

Beware of Gimmicks

There is a thin distinction between the practical inventions and gimmicks in the field of traeger smokers. Companies want to stand out above the rest because of increasing competition between manufacturers.

That's not to say all the features are just gimmicks and should be rejected as such. In the end, you have to worry about whether the traeger smoker apps are of particular value to you.

If the feature is something that you'd consider helpful, is it included at the expense of other, more important things like traeger use or durability?

However, if you live in a cold climate and it freezes outdoors, being able to control your cook from inside your warm home may be an appealing feature. If that's the case, then Davy Crockett of Green Mountain Grills might be your ally right up there.

Customer Service

As expected, Awesome Ribs has excellent customer service value advice, particularly for traeger grills.

A dedicated customer service team will likely exist by buying from a more significant, established company. It also means that if you need their help the company will probably be down the path for around a few years.

A smaller business will provide more intimate and consistent support on the flipside and your traeger grill concept really would be familiar to the people you approach

You won't figure out if the company fits in when it comes to consumer care until you pose queries and provide straightforward answers.

Price

Traeger grills vary considerably in size. Others will save you several hundred dollars and some will cost you thousands of dollars. A word of advice: Do not compare a cheap cooker with a good cooker for results.

A cheap cooker will save you early on, but if it continues to rust, after a few years you do not get a good warranty, and the customer service does not match, you may spend more cash in the long run.

On the other hand, if you bought all of the bells and whistles but didn't use them, you'll have wasted your hard-earned cash when a cooker that costs less would probably have done the trick.

Please check any of the above information before acquiring a cooker. See what you can and ask certain questions. Then, what you must do is love your fresh cooker!

Given the wide price range, it's important to decide if you want to buy a traeger smoker. Going through a guide is definitely an ideal way of ensuring you have not forgotten anything.

The Pros and Cons of Purchasing a Smoker with a Traeger

Because of its convenience and versatility, most people choose a traeger-style smoker. Just like a cigarette, you offer:

- Easy temperature regulation—Some traeger smokers require you to dial up to five degrees at temperature and the device is doing an outstanding job of holding the temperature constant.

Mastering Your Traeger Grill

The grill is the cooking system in which the food rests on bars, of different shapes and sizes, and, under these, the fuel in the form of firewood or coal heats at the same time the iron and the food that, little by little, is cooking.

A very essential aspect to consider when choosing a grill is the type of bar that can be round, in V, or square.

The round bar is the most generous with the product since when falling on the embers the fat of the product that we are cooking generates a cloud of smoke that aromatizes it. This can indeed raise the flame, but if we know how to handle it, the result is superior from the gastronomic point of view.

The V-bar, on the other hand, is easier to handle, since it picks up the fat that releases the food to a grease trap and it is more difficult for flames to be generated, but instead we lose in aromas. It is a system that is widely used in hospitality, since it allows cooking more quickly and without problems, but does not make much sense for a domestic grill.

Apart from the type of bar, which can be chosen in most models, there are fixed, semi-fixed, and portable grills.

If we have a large garden, we may be interested in installing a working grill, which can be found in different sizes from 100 euros (although a good one, for 5 or 6 people, does not fall below 300). These are modeling whose installation is more complex, but they are a good option in country houses where there is adequate space to install it. However, these are less versatile instruments and whose purchase is made almost as a function of the available space.

The semi-fixed grills are prefabricated structures designed to cram in a reserved space for these. They usually also have a drawer to collect the ashes. It is a good option if there is adequate space to install it and we do not want to get involved with a grill that is much more expensive.

The Barbecue

The barbecue is simply a grill with a lid, an additive that at first glance may not be decisive but that makes the invention a much more complex kitchen system, because, if it is lowered, it transforms it into an oven that cooks food from the controlled form. Also, thanks to the lid, the barbecue serves to smoke food, both cold and hot, and makes the instrument much safer, because if you have to leave the fire for any reason just lower this and close the shot to stay calm.

The barbecue is, in fact, a relatively recent invention. In 1950, George Stephen, known as the Newton of the barbecues, had a party to inaugurate his new house, he did not know how to control the fire of his charcoal grill and the food was scorched. That was when he thought about creating an improved grill.

There is nothing like cooking open flame food. The techniques are simple, cleaning is easy and grilled food tastes amazing.

Fundamentals

Choosing Smoker

The major and foremost step is to choose a smoker. You can invest in any type of smoker: charcoal smoker, gas smoker, or an electric smoker. A charcoal smoker runs for a long time and maintain steadier heat in the smoker and give meat pure flavors. A good choice for beginner cooks for smoking meat is a gas smoker where there is no need to monitor temperature but it comes with a downside that meat won't have much flavor compared to charcoal. On the other hand, the simplest, easiest, and popular smoker is an electric smoker. Cooking with an electric smoker involves only two-step: turn it on, put meat in it, and walk away.

Choosing Fuel

Wood chips add a unique flavor to the meat, therefore, select that wood chips that would enhance the taste of meat. Some wood chips have a stronger flavor; some have mild while others are just enough to be alone for smoking. Check out the segment titled "types of smoker wood" to get to know and decide on chips of wood that will complement your meat.

Type of Smoking Method

You have two choices to smoke meat, either using wet smoking, dry smoking, liquid smoke, or water smoking. Read the part "The core difference between cold and hot smoking" to find out the differences between each. In addition, go through the smoking meat portion in the unit "the difference between barbecuing a meat and smoking it".

Soaking Chips of Wood

Wood chips need to soak in order to last longer for fueling smoking. The reason is that dry wood burns quickly and this means adding more fuel to the smoker which can result in dry smoked meat. There isn't any need of using wood chips when smoking for a shorter time. Prepare wood chips by soaking them in water for at least 4 hours before starting smoking. Then drain chips and wrap and seal them in aluminum foil. Use a toothpick or fork for poking holes into the wood chips bag.

Set Smoker

Each type of smoker has its own way to start smoking. For wood or charcoal smokers, first, light up half of the charcoals and wait until their flame goes down. Then add remaining charcoal and wood chips if using. Wait until they are lighted and giving heat completely, then push charcoal aside and place the meat on the other side of the grilling grate. This is done to make sure that meat is indirectly smoked over low heat. Continue adding charcoal and soaked wood chips into the smoker.

For gas/propane or electric smoker, just turn it on according to manufacturer guidelines and then add soaked wood chips into chip holder and fill water receptacle if a smoker has one. Either make use of the incorporated thermostat or buy your own to monitor the internal temperature of the smoker. When the smoker reaches to desired preheated temperature, add meat to it.

Selecting Meat for Smoking

Choose the type of meat that tastes good with a smoky flavor. Following meat goes well for smoking.

- Beef: ribs, brisket, and corned beef.
- Pork: spare ribs, roast, shoulder, and ham.
- Poultry: whole chicken, whole turkey, and big game hens.
- Seafood: Salmon, scallops, trout, and lobster.

Getting Meat Ready

Prepare meat according to the recipe. Sometimes meat is cured, marinated, or simply seasoned with the rub. These preparation methods ensure smoked meat turns out flavorful, tender, and extremely juicy.

Brine is a solution to treating poultry, pork, or ham. It involves dissolving brine ingredients in water poured into a huge container and then adding meat to it. Then let soak for at least 8 hours and after that, rinse it well and pat dry before you begin smoking.

Rubs are commonly used to treat beef, poultry, or ribs. They are actually a combination of salt and many spices, rubbed generously all over the meat. Then the meat is left to rest for at least 2 hours or more before smoking it.

Before smoking meat, make sure it is at room temperature. This ensures the meat is cooked evenly and reaches its internal temperature at the end of smoking time.

Placing Meat into The Smoker

Don't place the meat directly over the heat into the smoker because the main purpose of smoking is cooking meat at low temperatures. Set aside your fuel on one side of the smoker and place the meat on the other side and let cook.

Smoking time: The smoking time of meat depends on the internal temperature. For this, use a meat thermometer and insert it into the thickest part of the meat. The smoking time also varies with the size of the meat. Check recipes to determine the exact smoking time for the meat.

Basting Meat

Some recipes call for brushing the meat with thin solutions, sauces, or marinade. This step not only makes meat better in taste, but it also helps to maintain moisture in meat through the smoking process. Read the recipe to check out if basting is necessary.

Taking out meat: When the meat reaches its desired internal temperature, remove it from the smoker. Generally, poultry should be removed from the smoker when its internal temperature reaches 165°F. For ground meats, ham, and pork, the internal temperature should be 160°F. 145°F is the internal temperature for chops, roast, and steaks.

Maintenance

Traeger grills are incredibly convenient. But it is important to keep in mind that you are still playing with live fire. You'll want to be prepared to deal with accidents and other issues. Each traeger grill smoker's owner's manual has official information on safety, troubleshooting, and maintenance.

If you are a new traeger grill owner, the first step in safety is to follow the manufacturer's instructions for the initial firing of the grill. This will burn off any manufacturing oils and bits of Styrofoam packaging that may remain on cooking surfaces.

Never use your traeger grill in an enclosed area. Dangerous gasses can accumulate quickly. Grilling inside your home is obviously a smoky and bad idea, but also do not grill in enclosed porches and tents, which are, also, dangerous.

To stay safe (and be able to enjoy your delicious smoker results), keep the following safety tips in mind at all times.

Safety 101

- Have a dedicated fire extinguisher for your grill area (and another for your kitchen).

- Never attempt to move a hot grill.

- Follow the manufacturer's standard starting, preheating, and shutdown procedures. These steps will allow you to safely prime and ignite and later extinguish and clear your auger and fire pot. The procedures help prevent the unsafe accumulation of traegers in the fire pot.

- The grill will produce airborne hot embers, so keep kids, pets, flammable liquids, and vinyl siding a safe distance away from it for the entire cooking process.

- Don't smoke with strange wood, particularly traegers that were not produced specifically for cooking. Non–food-safe traegers can be comprised of scrap wood. Construction scrap wood is often treated with toxic chemicals and other undesirable finishes that you wouldn't want to ingest.

- Traeger grill smoker manufacturers don't want you to leave these cookers on for hours fully unattended. They express this in the owner's manual fine print. You'll also notice that in sales photos, they play it safe—the cook is always in eyeshot across the yard, relaxing in a chaise, or in the kitchen keeping the cooker in the view from the window.

- Never operate your traeger grill in the rain. Remember, your grill relies on electricity to operate, and electric machines should never get wet. Plus, traegers are sensitive to moisture and will swell, disintegrate, and make a mess when wet.

- Unplug your traeger grill when not in use, and avoid linking long extension cords. Even though the grill generates its heat with burning wood, you still have possible electricity dangers. Remember, too, that your traeger grill won't operate if you lose power.

- Accidents and mistakes happen all the time, but rest assured that your traeger grill is constructed with safety in mind and is safer to operate than charcoal and stick-burning smokers. This is because you don't have to add wood to the hot coals to stoke the fire manually. With a traeger grill, the small fire pot is tucked away inside the grill and stoked automatically thanks to the auger and the thermostat.

Troubleshooting Tips

If you feel like your grill is struggling to maintain heat, cold temperatures may be the culprit. Your traeger grill's thermostat should compensate and have your auger and fire pot work harder. Windy conditions can be a more sneaky problem. When possible, position your grill to avoid the direct wind. Specially constructed insulated grill covers are available from manufacturers (like Traeger) to combat exceptionally windy and cold conditions. It may seem odd for a grill to wear a sweater, but the nonflammable material can safely provide needed insulation in windy and extra-cold conditions.

Any smoker is susceptible to delayed cook times due to prying eyes. In fact, every time you open the cook chamber to peek, it can add take up to 15 minutes to regain temperatures. A right traeger grill's thermostat can combat this better than most other types of smokers, but if you think your cook times are longer than they should be, it's worth evaluating. As the saying goes, "If you're looking', you aren't cooking'."

Occasional ash cleanup is necessary to keep your grill in profitable operation. Be sure to do your cleaning before the procedure, or at least 12 hours after any ignition.

A dependable power source is essential. Unlike charcoal and gas grills, traeger grills require electricity to stoke traegers into the fire pot. A blown fuse or any interruption in power will make your grill inoperable.

1. Maintenance Tips

Keep it clean. Your traeger grill requires little maintenance other than an occasional removal of ash from the fire pot. When fully cool, you can use a shop vac to remove excess ash in and around the fire pot and cook chamber. This is recommended after three to five cooks (or after exceptionally long cooks).

- Vacuum the areas in and around the hopper occasionally, as they can accumulate sawdust and traeger remnants after use.

- Clean your grill grate after each use. Porcelain-coated grates should be scrubbed with a nonmetallic brush to protect the porcelain finish.

- Use a cover when the grill is not in use to protect from bleaching sunlight, moisture, and nesting insects.

If you are having ignition or temperature problems, visually inspect the fire pot. Over time, the fire pot is the most commonly replaced part on traeger grills; due to intense heat and constant use, it is more susceptible to corrosion and wear. You can replace yours with any preferred stainless-steel fire pots.

Accessories

You can quickly adapt much of the kitchen and barbecue gear you already own for smoking. But let's face it: We pit masters love our toys. Here's a list of my favorite tools and gadgets. They're almost as drool-worthy as the meat you can smoke with them.

Must-Haves

- THERMOMETER: Everyone needs a good meat thermometer. Old-school analog meat thermometers are fine, but I have noticed a significant price drop recently in quality, instant-read digital thermometers. Ten bucks on Amazon will get you a reliable probe you can use with confidence.

- SPRAY BOTTLE: Look at Walmart or in your supermarket's garden supply area to find food-safe empty plastic spray bottles for thin sauces. As with injectors, you need to keep the liquid free of lumps and chunky spices that will clog the inner tube. But the nice thing about these bottles is that you can throw them in the dishwasher and reuse them.

- INJECTOR: These tools, resembling a doctor's syringe, make it possible to marinate meat from the inside out. Your inner caveman will be tempted to buy a commercial-grade, heavy-duty injector, but I've always had success with the cheap plastic turkey injectors found in the grocery store.

- FIRE EXTINGUISHER: This may seem silly, especially when we're talking about smoking at low temperatures, but I believe it's worth having two: one small fire extinguisher for the kitchen and one near the patio. But you probably already have a kitchen fire extinguisher—right?

- GLOVES: I like waterproof and heat-resistant grill gloves. Use them to grab meat directly off the grate and start to pull apart pork butts by hand.
- HEAVY-DUTY ALUMINUM FOIL: You can find plain old heavy-duty aluminum foil at most large grocery stores. Use it to wrap whole roasts, line drip pans and

More Toys

- NONSTICK GRILL MATS: These heat-resistant, flexible mesh mats help make quick work of smoker cleanup. Unlike a layer of foil, which prohibits the flow of smoke and air, the mesh allows the bottom of your meat to get just as much smoke as the top and sides.
- PERFORATED PIZZA SCREEN: In a pinch, use 12-inch pizza screens instead of grill mats. You can get them for a few bucks each at stores like Kitchen Collection and Bed Bath & Beyond or on Amazon. They're rigid, easy to handle, reusable, and dishwasher safe. trays, tent meats during the resting phase, and wrap food for storage.
- GRILL BRUSH/SCRAPER: Use caution with wire grill brushes. The bristles sometimes fall out, and you don't want stray wires in your food. Another danger is the possibility of scratching porcelain-coated grill grates. Instead, use a high-temperature plastic grill brush, like the ones made by Char-Broil. Or try my new favorite grilling tool, the Great Scrape.
- RIB RACK: Smoker grates are often limited in size. If you're working with a round grate and a domed lid, you'll want a simple rib rack to maximize every square inch of the grill.

How to Clean Your Grill

Traeger grills are easy to clean compare to similar grills. You would need to clean it every five uses, which is wonderful. Traditional grills can be a chore to clean and can get pretty grimy quickly. Luckily, the Traeger's design allows you to get your grill ready for the next cook-out in few simple steps.

1. Open the grill lid and wipe the grates with a paper towel or damp cloth. If your grates have more residue, you can use a grill mark brush instead. Use a scraper to remove debris at the back wall of the grill then let all the dirt fall on the bottom of the drip tray.

2. Brush or wipe the inside of the smoke exhaust and empty the grease bucket.

3. Take out the drip pan and replace it with a fresh aluminum foil.

4. Siphon the ash beneath the heat deflector and on the inside of the fire pot using a vacuum.

5. Use a grease cleaner or soapy water on a spray bottle for cleaning the exterior of the grill. Spray it while carefully avoiding the electronic controls. Leave it on for 1 minute, then wipe it down with a clean cloth.

More Tips:

- Make sure that the grill has completely cooled down before cleaning.

- Take the opportunity to visually inspect the parts when cleaning to have them in excellent working order.
- Follow the top to bottom cleaning method.
- Empty the traeger hopper and vacuum the insides to get any ash or dust.
- You may need to clean the temperature probes when they get grubby. Do these gently by using a clean damp cloth.
- Be careful when drawing out the grate since you may damage or scrape the temperature probe.
- Always replace the foil every cook cycle to keep the smoke flavors pristine and avoid getting any particulates from previous cooks sticking to what you are currently grilling.
- Use grease liners or aluminum foil for the grease bucket for easy cleanup. Never pour the grease down the drain since this will clog your pipes.

Cooking Temperatures, Times, and Doneness

As a general guide, below are different temperatures and the time required for the following food items.

Fish and Seafood:

- White fish and Salmon can be grilled at 400–450° F for 5–8 minutes on each side or until flaky
- Steamed lobster can be cooked at 200–225° F for 15 minutes per pound of lobster.
- Scallops cook at 190° F for 1–1.5 hours
- Shrimps require 400–450° F for 3–5 minutes on each side

Pork:

- Pork ribs may be smoked at 275° F for 3–6 hours

- Pork loin cooks at 400° F until the internal temperature reaches 145–150° F
- Pulled pork butt may be cooked at 225–250° F and until the internal temperature reaches 205° F
- Bacon and sausages cook at 425° F for 7 minutes on each side or until cooked

Beef:

- Beef short ribs may be cooked at 225–250° F for 4–6 hours until the meat easily pulls off from the bone
- Beef brisket cooks at 250° F for 4 hours then covered with foil to cook for another 4 hours or more
- Medium rare beef tenderloin cooks at 225–250° F for 3 hours
- Beef jerky requires a low heat setting for 4–5 hours

Poultry:

- Whole chicken cooks at 400° F until internal temperature reaches 165° F
- Chicken breast requires 400° F and 15 minutes on each side
- Pheasant cooks at 200° F for 2–3 hours until internal temperature reaches 160° F
- Smoked turkey requires a temperature of 180–225° F for 10–12 hours or until the internal temperature is 165° F.

Chicken Recipes

1. Hellfire Chicken Wings

Preparation Time: 30 minutes

Cooking Time: 6 Hours

Servings: 1

Ingredients:

- For Hellfire chicken wings
- 3 lbs. chicken wings
- 2 tbsp. vegetable oil
- For the rub
- 1 tsp. onion powder
- 1 tbsp. paprika
- 1 tsp. celery seed
- 1 tsp. salt
- 1 tsp. cayenne pepper
- 1 tsp. freshly ground black pepper
- 1 tsp. granulated garlic
- 2 tsp. brown sugar:
- For the sauce
- 2–4 thinly sliced crosswise jalapeno poppers
- 2 tbsp. butter; unsalted
- ½ cup hot sauce
- ½ cup cilantro leaves

Directions:

1. Take the chicken wings and cut off the tips and discard them.

2. Now cut each of the wings into two separate pieces through the joint.
3. Move this in a large mixing bowl and pour oil right over it.
4. For the rub: Take a small-sized bowl and add sugar, black pepper, paprika, onion powder, salt, celery seed, cayenne, and granulated garlic in it.
5. Now sprinkle this mixture over the chicken and toss it gently to coat the wings thoroughly.
6. Put the smoker to preheat by putting the temperature to 350°F.
7. Grill the wings for approximately 40 minutes or till the time the skin turns golden brown and you feel that it has cooked through. Make sure to turn it once when you are halfway.
8. For the sauce: Take a small saucepan and melt the butter by keeping the flame on medium-low heat. Now add jalapenos to it and cook for 3 minutes, stir cilantro along with a hot sauce.
9. Now, pour this freshly made sauce over the wings and toss it to coat well.
10. Serve and enjoy.

Nutrition:

- Carbs: 27 g
- Protein: 19 g
- Sodium: 65 mg
- Cholesterol: 49 mg

2. Buffalo Chicken Thighs

Preparation Time: 30 minutes

Cooking Time: 6 Hours

Servings: 1

Ingredients:

- 4–6 skinless, boneless chicken thighs
- Pork and poultry rub
- 4 tbsp. butter
- 1 cup sauce; buffalo wing
- Bleu cheese crumbles
- Ranch dressing

Directions:

1. Set the grill to preheat by keeping the temperature to 450°F and keeping the lid closed.
2. Now season the chicken thighs with the poultry rub and then place it on the grill grate.
3. Cook it for 8 to 10 minutes while making sure to flip it once midway.
4. Now take a small saucepan and cook the wing sauce along with butter by keeping the flame on medium heat. Make sure to stir in between to avoid lumps.
5. Now take the cooked chicken and dip it into the wing sauce and the butter mix. Make sure to coat both the sides in an even manner.

6. Take the chicken thighs that have been sauced to the grill and then cook for further 15 minutes. Do so until the internal temperature reads 175°F.
7. Sprinkle bleu cheese and drizzle the ranch dressing.
8. Serve and enjoy.

Nutrition:

- Carbs: 29 g
- Protein: 19 g
- Sodium: 25 mg
- Cholesterol: 19 mg

3. Sweet and Sour Chicken Drumsticks

Preparation Time: 30 minutes

Cooking Time: 2 Hours

Servings: 1

Ingredients:

- 8 pieces chicken drumsticks
- 2 tbsp. rice wine vinegar
- 3 tbsp. brown sugar:
- 1 cup ketchup
- ¼ cup soy sauce
- Minced garlic
- 2 tbsp. honey
- 1 tbsp. sweet heat rub
- Minced ginger
- ½ lemon, juiced
- ½ lime, juiced

Directions:

1. Take a mixing bowl and add soy sauce along with brown sugar, ketchup, lemon, rice wine vinegar, sweet heat rub, honey, ginger, and garlic.
2. Now keep half of the mixture for dipping sauce and therefore set it aside.
3. Take the leftover half and pour it into a plastic bag that can be re-sealed.

4. Now add drumsticks to it and then seal the bag again.

5. Refrigerate it for 4 to 12 hours.

6. Take out the chicken from the bag and discard the marinade.

7. Fire the grill and set the temperature to 225°F.

8. Now smoke the chicken over indirect heat for 2 to 3 hours a make sure to turn it once or twice.

9. Add more glaze if needed.

10. Remove it from the grill and let it stand aside for 10 minutes.

11. Add more sauce or keep it as a dipping sauce.

12. Serve and enjoy.

Nutrition:

-   Carbs: 29 g
-   Protein: 19 g
-   Sodium: 25 mg
-   Cholesterol: 19 mg

4. Beer-Braised Chicken Tacos with Jalapenos Relish

Preparation Time: 30 minutes

Cooking Time: 3 Hours

Servings: 1

Ingredients:

- For the braised chicken
- 2 lbs. chicken thighs; boneless, skinless
- ½ small-sized diced onion
- 1 de-seeded and chopped jalapeno
- 1 (12 oz.) can Modelo beer
- 1 tbsp. olive oil
- 1 EA chipotle Chile in adobo
- 1 clove minced garlic
- 4 tbsp. adobo sauce
- 1 tsp. chili powder
- 1 tsp. garlic powder
- 1 tsp. salt
- 1 tsp. black pepper
- Juice 2 limes
- For the tacos
- 8–12 tortillas; small flour
- Hot sauce
- Cilantro
- Cotija cheese
- For the jalapeno relish

- ¼ cup finely diced red onion
- 3 seeded and diced jalapenos
- 1 clove minced garlic
- ⅓ cup water
- 1 tbsp. Sugar:
- ⅔ cup white wine vinegar
- 1 tbsp. salt
- For pickled cabbage
- 2 cups red cabbage; shredded
- ½ cup white wine vinegar
- 1 tbsp. Sugar:
- 1 tbsp. salt

Directions:

1. For the jalapeño relish: take all the ingredients and mix them in a non-reactive dish and then keep it aside to be used.
2. For the pickled cabbage: take another non-reactive dish and mix all its respective ingredients and keep it aside
3. Now, transfer both the relish along with the pickled cabbage to your refrigerator and allow it to see for a couple of hours or even overnight if you so desire
4. Take the chicken thighs and season them with an adequate amount of salt and pepper
5. Take a Dutch oven and keep the flame over medium-high heat. Heat 1 tbsp. of olive oil in it
6. Now place the chicken thighs skin side down and brown
7. Remove them from the heat and then set them aside

8. Now, add 1 tbsp. of butter and keep the flame to medium-high
9. When the butter has melted, add jalapeno along with onion and sauté it for 3 to 5 minutes until they turn translucent
10. Add minced garlic to it and sauté it for 30 more seconds
11. Now add adobo sauce along with lime juice, chili powder, and chipotle chile.
12. Add the chicken thighs in the oven and pour in the beer
13. Now set the grill to pre-heat by keeping the temperature to 350°F
14. Place the oven on the grill and let it braise for 30 minutes
15. Remove the chicken from the braising liquid and slowly shred it
16. For the tacos: place the shredded part of chicken on the tortillas. Top it with jalapeno relish along with cotija, cabbage, and cilantro, and pour the hot sauce
17. Serve and enjoy

Nutrition:

- Carbs: 29 g
- Protein: 19 g
- Sodium: 25 mg
- Cholesterol: 19 mg

5. Smoked Teriyaki Chicken Wings with Sesame Dressing

Preparation Time: 30 minutes

Cooking Time: 4 Hours

Servings: 1

Ingredients:

- Chicken wings
- For the homemade Teriyaki Glaze:
- $^2/_3$ cup mirin
- 2 tbsp. minced ginger
- 3 tbsp. cornstarch
- 2 tbsp. rice vinegar
- 1 cup soy sauce
- $^1/_3$ cup brown sugar:
- 8 minced garlic cloves
- 2 tsp. sesame oil
- 3 tbsp. water
- For creamy sesame dressing:
- 1 green onion, chopped
- $^1/_2$ cup mayonnaise
- $^1/_4$ cup rice wine vinegar
- 1 tsp. ground garlic
- 1 tbsp. soy sauce
- 2 tbsp. sesame oil
- $^1/_2$ tsp. ground ginger
- 1 tsp. siracha

- 2 tbsp. maple syrup
- Salt and pepper to taste

Directions:

1. Use the light traegers for the sake of getting the smokey flavor
2. Set the grill to smoke mode by keeping the temperature to 225°F
3. Now trim the wings and make them into drumettes and season with sea salt and black pepper
4. Smoke them for nearly 45 minutes
5. For the teriyaki glaze
6. Mince both garlic and ginger by using a tsp. of sesame oil
7. Then mix all the ingredients except for cornstarch and water
8. Take a pan and boil cornstarch and water on low heat
9. Simmer for 15 minutes and then when done, mix it with an immersion blender
10. Now add cornstarch and water and stir it until it has mixed well
11. Add this mix to the teriyaki glaze and mix it well until it thickens. Set it aside
12. For the creamy dressing
13. Take a blender and blend all the ingredients thoroughly until you get a smooth mixture
14. Now set the grill for direct flame grilling and put the temperature to medium
15. Grill the wings for approx. 10 minutes

16. The internal temperature should reach 165°F when you remove the wings from the grill

17. Toss them in the glaze when done

18. Sprinkle some sesame seeds along with green onion

19. Serve hot and spicy

Nutrition:

- Carbs: 39 g
- Protein: 29 g
- Sodium: 15 mg
- Cholesterol: 19 mg

6. Spiced Lemon Chicken

Preparation Time: 30 minutes

Cooking Time: 5 Hours

Servings: 1

Ingredients:

- 1 whole chicken
- 4 cloves minced garlic
- Zest 2 fresh lemons
- 1 tbsp. olive oil
- 1 tbsp. smoked paprika
- 1 ½ tsp. salt
- ½ tsp. black pepper
- ½ tsp. dried oregano
- 1 tbsp. ground cumin

Directions:

1. Preheat the grill by pushing the temperature to 375°F
2. Now take the chicken and spatchcock it by cutting it on both the sides right from the backbone to the tail via the neck
3. Lay it flat and push it down on the breastbone. This would break the ribs
4. Take all the leftover ingredients in a bowl except ½ tsp. of salt and crush them to make a smooth rub
5. Spread this rub evenly over the chicken making sure that it seeps right under the skin

6. Now place the chicken on the grill grates and let it cook for an hour until the internal temperature reads 165°F

7. Let it rest for 10 minutes

8. Serve and enjoy

Nutrition:

- Carbs: 39 g
- Protein: 29 g
- Sodium: 15 mg
- Cholesterol: 19 mg

7. Grilled Chicken in Traegers

Preparation Time: 10 minutes

Cooking Time: 30 minutes

Servings: 8

Ingredients:

- Whole chicken (4–5 lbs.)
- Grilled chicken mix

Directions:

1. Preheat the traeger grill with the 'smoke' option for 5 minutes.
2. Preheat another 10 minutes and keep the temperature on high until it reaches 450°F.
3. Use baker's twine to tie the chicken's legs together.
4. Keep the breast side up when you place the chicken in the grill.
5. Grill for 70 minutes. Do not open the grill during this process.
6. Check the temperature of your grilled chicken. Make sure it is 165 degrees. If not, leave the chicken in for longer.
7. Carefully take the chicken out of the grill.
8. Set aside for 15 minutes.
9. Cut and serve.

Nutrition: Carbs: 0 g Protein: 107 g Fat: 0 g Sodium: 320 mg Cholesterol: 346 mg

Beef Recipes

8. Smoked Longhorn Cowboy Tri-Tip

Preparation Time: 15 minutes

Cooking Time: 4 hours

Servings: 7

Ingredients:

- 3 lb. tri-tip roast
- ⅛ cup coffee, ground
- ¼ cup Traeger beef rub

Directions:

1. Preheat the grill to 180°F with the lid closed for 15 minutes.
2. Meanwhile, rub the roast with coffee and beef rub. Place the roast on the grill grate and smoke for 3 hours.
3. Remove the roast from the grill and double wrap it with foil. Increase the temperature to 275°F.
4. Return the meat to the grill and let cook for 90 minutes or until the internal temperature reaches 135°F.
5. Remove from the grill, unwrap it and let rest for 10 minutes before serving.

Nutrition:

- Calories: 245
- Fat: 14g
- Protein: 23g
- Sugar: 0g
- Fiber: 0g
- Sodium: 80mg

9. Traeger Grill Teriyaki Beef Jerky

Preparation Time: 15 minutes

Cooking Time: 5 hours

Servings: 10

Ingredients:

- 3 cups soy sauce
- 2 cups brown Sugar
- 3 garlic cloves
- 2-inch ginger knob, peeled and chopped
- 1 tbsp. sesame oil
- 4 lb. beef, skirt steak

Directions:

1. Place all the ingredients except the meat in a food processor. Pulse until well mixed.
2. Trim any excess fat from the meat and slice into ¼ inch slices. Add the steak with the marinade into a Ziploc bag and let marinate for 12–24 hours in a fridge.
3. Set the traeger grill to smoke and let preheat for 5 minutes.
4. Arrange the steaks on the grill leaving a space between each. Let smoke for 5 hours.
5. Remove the steak from the grill and serve when warm.

Nutrition: Calories: 80 Fat: 1g Protein: 11g Sugar: 6g Fiber: 0g Sodium: 390mg

10.Grilled Butter Basted Rib-eye

Preparation Time: 20 minutes **Cooking Time:** 20 minutes

Servings: 4

Ingredients:

- 2 rib-eye steaks, bone-in
- Salt to taste
- Pepper to taste
- 4 tbsp. butter, unsalted

Directions:

1. Mix steak, salt, and pepper in a Ziploc bag. Seal the bag and mix until the beef is well coated. Ensure you get as much air as possible from the Ziploc bag.
2. Set the traeger grill temperature to high with closed lid for 15 minutes. Place a cast-iron into the grill.
3. Place the steaks on the hottest spot of the grill and cook for 5 minutes with the lid closed.
4. Open the lid and add butter to the skillet. When it's almost melted place the steak on the skillet with the grilled side up.
5. Cook for 5 minutes while busting the meat with butter. Close the lid and cook until the internal temperature is 130°F.
6. Remove the steak from the skillet and let rest for 10 minutes before enjoying with the reserved butter.

Nutrition: Calories: 745 Fat: 65g Protein: 35g Sugar: 0g Fiber: 0g

11. Traeger smoked Brisket

Preparation Time: 20 minutes **Cooking Time:** 9 hours

Servings: 6

Ingredients:

- 2 tbsp. garlic powder
- 2 tbsp. onion powder
- 2 tbsp. paprika
- 2 tbsp. chili powder
- ⅓ cup salt
- ⅓ cup black pepper
- 12 lb. whole packer brisket, trimmed
- 1-½ cup beef broth

Directions:

1. Set your traeger temperature to 225°F. Let preheat for 15 minutes with the lid closed.
2. Meanwhile, mix garlic, onion, paprika, chili, salt, and pepper in a mixing bowl.
3. Season the brisket generously on all sides. Place the meat on the grill with the fat side down and let it cool until the internal temperature reaches 160°F. Remove the meat from the grill and double wrap it with foil. Return it to the grill and cook until the internal temperature reaches 204°F. Remove from grill, unwrap the brisket and let rest for 15 minutes. Slice and serve.

Nutrition: Calories: 270 Fat: 20g Protein: 20g Sugar: 1g Fiber: 0g Sodium: 1220mg

12. Traeger Smoked Rib-eye Steaks

Preparation Time: 15 minutes

Cooking Time: 35 minutes

Servings: 1

Ingredients:

- 2-inch thick rib-eye steaks
- Steak rub of choice

Directions:

1. Preheat your traeger grill to low smoke.
2. Sprinkle the steak with your favorite steak rub and place it on the grill. Let it smoke for 25 minutes.
3. Remove the steak from the grill and set the temperature to 400°F.
4. Return the steak to the grill and sear it for 5 minutes on each side.
5. Cook until the desired temperature is achieved; 125°F-rare, 145°F-Medium, and 165°F.-Well done.
6. Wrap the steak with foil and let rest for 10 minutes before serving. Enjoy.

Nutrition:

- Calories: 225, Fat: 10.4g,
- Protein: 32.5g,
- Sugar: 0g,
- Fiber: 0g,
- Sodium: 63mg,

13.Smoked Trip Tip with Java Chophouse

Preparation Time: 10 minutes

Cooking Time: 90 minutes

Servings: 4

Ingredients:

- 2 tbsp. olive oil
- 2 tbsp. java chophouse seasoning
- 3 lb. trip tip roast, fat cap and silver skin removed

Directions:

1. Startup your traeger grill and smoker and set the temperature to 225°F.
2. Rub the roast with olive oil and seasoning then place it on the smoker rack.
3. Smoke until the internal temperature is 140°F.
4. Remove the tri-tip from the smoker and let rest for 10 minutes before serving. Enjoy.

Nutrition:

- Calories: 270,
- Fat: 7g,
- Protein: 23g,
- Sugar: 0g,
- Fiber: 0g,
- Sodium: 47mg,

Pork Recipes

14.Florentine Ribeye Pork Loin

Preparation Time: 30 minutes

Cooking Time: 60 to 75 minutes

Servings: 6 to 8

Ingredients:

- 1 (3-pound) boneless ribeye pork loin roast
- 4 tbsp. extra-virgin olive oil, divided
- 2 tbsp. Pork Dry Rub or your favorite pork seasoning
- 4 bacon slices
- 6 cups fresh spinach
- 1 small red onion, diced
- 6 cloves garlic, cut into thin slivers
- ¾ cup shredded mozzarella cheese

Directions:

1. Trim away any abundance fat and silver skin.
2. Butterfly the pork loin or approach your butcher to butterfly it for you. There are numerous phenomenal recordings online with nitty-gritty directions on the various systems for butterflying a loin roast.
3. Rub 2 tbsp. of the olive oil on each side of the butterflied roast and season the two sides with the rub.
4. Cook the bacon in a large skillet over medium heat. Disintegrate and set aside. Reserve the bacon fat.
5. Grill the pork loin for 60 to 75 minutes, or until the internal temperature at the thickest part arrives at 140°F.

6. Rest the pork loin under a free foil tent for 15 minutes before cutting contrary to what would be expected.

Nutrition:

- Calories: 365
- Protein: 32.1 g
- Fat: 22 g

15.Naked St. Louis Ribs

Preparation Time: 30 minutes **Cooking Time:** 5 to 6 hours

Servings: 6 to 8

Ingredients:

Traeger: Hickory, Apple

- 3 St. Louis–style pork rib racks
- 1 cup in addition to 1 tbsp. Jan's Original Dry Rub or your preferred pork rub

Directions:

1. Remove the membrane on the underside of the rib racks by embedding a spoon handle between the membrane and rib bones. Get the membrane with a paper towel and gradually dismantle it down the rack to remove.
2. Rub the two sides of the ribs with a liberal measure of the rub.
3. Arrange the traeger smoker-grill for non-direct cooking and preheat to 225°F utilizing hickory or apple traegers.
4. In the event of utilizing a rib rack, place the ribs in the rack on the grill grates. Else you can utilize Teflon-covered fiberglass tangles or place the ribs directly on the grill grates.
5. Smoke the ribs at 225°F for 5 to 6 hours with hickory traegers until the internal temperature, at the thickest part of the ribs, arrives at 185°F to190°F.
6. Rest the ribs under a free foil tent for 10 minutes before cutting and serving.

Nutrition: Calories: 241 Protein: 23.6 g Fat: 13 g

16.Buttermilk Pork Sirloin Roast

Preparation Time: 20 minutes

Cooking Time: 3 to 3½ hours

Servings: 4 to 6

Ingredients:

Traeger: Apple, Cherry

- 1 (3 to 3½-pound) pork sirloin roast

Directions:

1. Trim all fat and silver skin from the pork roast.
2. Place the roast and buttermilk brine in a 1-gallon sealable plastic sack or brining holder.
3. Refrigerate medium-term, turning the roast like clockwork whenever the situation allows.
4. Remove the brined pork sirloin roast from the brine and pat dry with a paper towel.
5. Supplement a meat probe into the thickest part of the roast.
6. Design the traeger smoker-grill for non-direct cooking and preheat to 225°F utilizing apple or cherry traegers.
7. Smoke the roast until the internal temperature arrives at 145°F, 3 to 3 and a half hours.
8. Rest the roast under a free foil tent for 15 minutes, at that point cut contrary to what would be expected.

Nutrition: Calories: 311 Protein: 25 g Fat: 18 g

17.Pierna Criolla

Preparation Time: 12 Hours

Cooking Time: 2.5 Hours

Servings: 18

Ingredients:

- 1 8-lbs. pork shoulder
- 8 slices bacon
- ½ lb. ham
- 1 bottle Malta
- 1 cup guava shells
- 1 cup Mojo (pg. 125)
- 1 cup prunes
- 4 tbsp. Adobo Spices
- 2 cups brown sugar
- 2 tbsp. sea salt

Directions:

1. Debone and flatten meat so that it may be rolled.
2. If the pork shoulder is very fatty, a small amount may be removed.
3. Score fat well and marinate for a minimum of 12 hours in the Mojo, and Adobo.
4. Sear both sides of roast on a very hot grate until dark brown and charred in spots, using apple-traegers for a smoky flavor.
5. Remove roast to cutting board, and line unrolled roast with ham slices, bacon slices, prunes, and guava shells. Roll meat

carefully to keep the filling inside. Tie firmly with a butcher cord.

6. Cover with brown Sugar: and ½ bottle of Malta.

7. Cook for one hour in the traeger smoker at 325°F.

8. At this point, turn the meat, cover with remaining Malta and cook for an extra hour, or until you reach a meat temperature of 180°F.

9. Let cool for at least 30 minutes and cut into fine slices. Pour the drippings over the meat after slicing the meat.

10. These ingredients can be found at most Hispanic grocery stores.

Nutrition:

- Calories: 83
- Carbs: 19g
- Fat: 0g
- Protein: 3g

18.Sweet & Spicy Pork Kabobs

Preparation Time: 24 Hours

Cooking Time: 10 minutes

Servings: 6

Ingredients:

- 2 lbs. boneless pork, 1-inch cubes
- ¾ cup olive oil
- 1 tbsp. Worcestershire sauce
- 1 tsp. dried thyme
- 2 tsp. black pepper
- ½ tsp. cayenne
- ¾ cup cider vinegar
- ¼ cup sugar
- 4 tbsp. lemon juice
- 1 tbsp. oregano
- 2 cloves garlic, minced
- 1 tsp. salt

Directions:

1. Mix together the first 11 ingredients, place in a sealable bag and refrigerate 24 hours: thread onto skewers.
2. Grill on high heat, basting with reserved marinade, for 4–5 minutes; turn and grill another 4–5 minutes.
3. Sprinkle with salt and serve.

Nutrition: Calories: 160 Carbs: 2g Fat: 5g Protein: 28g

19.Big Island Pork Kabobs

Preparation Time: 24 Hours

Cooking Time: 15 minutes

Servings: 6

Ingredients:

- 3 lbs. Pork tenderloin
- 3 cup margarita mix
- 3 clove garlic, minced
- 2 large bell peppers
- 4 lbs. whole mushrooms
- ¼ cup butter, softened
- 4 tsp. lime juice
- 1 tsp. Sugar:
- 3 tbsp. minced parsley

Directions:

1. Cut pork into 1-inch cubes, place in a sealable plastic bag; pour marinade over to cover. Marinate overnight.
2. Blend together the butter, lime juice, Splenda, and parsley; set aside.
3. Thread pork cubes onto skewers, alternating with mushrooms and pepper, cut into eighths.
4. Grill over high heat, basting with butter mixture, for 10–15 minutes, turning frequently. If you're using bamboo skewers, soak them in water 20–30 minutes before using.

Nutrition: Calories: 160 Carbs: 2g Fat: 5g Protein: 28g

20.   Asian Pork Sliders

Preparation Time: 24 Hours

Cooking Time: 15 minutes

Servings: 8

Ingredients:

- 2 lbs. ground pork
- 1 cup diced green onion
- 2 tsp. garlic powder
- 2 tbsp. soy sauce
- 2 tsp. brown sugar:
- 1 cup shredded lettuce
- 1 tsp. cornstarch
- Honey-mustard dressing
- 16 sesame rolls, split

Directions:

1. Mix all ingredients (except soy sauce) and form 16 equal patties. Brush each patty with soy sauce, and grill over high heat, turning once.
2. Serve with honey mustard and cucumber spears.
3. I like to chill the seasoned meat and then spread it on an oiled cutting board, using a rolling pin for an even ¼-inch thickness.   Then, I just grab a biscuit cutter, and voila...perfectly round sliders!

Nutrition: Calories: 280 Carbs: 31g Fat: 9g Protein: 26g

21.Luau Pork

Preparation Time: 12 Hours

Cooking Time: 12 Hours

Servings: 50

Ingredients:

- 2 boneless pork shoulders (6 lbs.)
- 2 cup hot water
- 3 Qtrs. gal Hawaiian Mojo
- 2 tbsp. seasoned salt
- ¼ cup Stubbs liquid smoke
- 4 tbsp. garlic powder
- ½ cup Adobo Criollo spices

Directions:

1. Marinate pork in Hawaiian Mojo overnight. Remove from marinade, pat dry, and inject each shoulder with 6-8ozs of remaining marinade.
2. Score pork on all sides, rub with salt, then brush with liquid smoke, and sprinkle with garlic. Wrap entirely in banana leaves, tie with string.
3. Heat one side of your traeger grill to high, covered.
4. Once preheated, place the butts on the "cool" side of the grill, roast 3 hours with oak traegers, and then remove banana leaves. Baste with mojo every 45 minutes throughout the rest of the cooking time. The shoulders should not be over any exposed flame.

5. Cover the grill and vent slightly. Slowly cook the shoulders for a total of 6 to 8 hours, until the meat is very tender, or you reach 195°F on the meat thermometer.

6. Chop the meat and then mix with a wash of ½ cup liquid smoke, 4 cups hot water, 1/4 cup Adobo Criollo spices, and 2 tbsp. seasoned salt.

7. Let that sit about 15 minutes, drain remaining liquid, and serve with Sweet Hawaiian Pork Sauce

Nutrition:

- Calories: 116
- Carbs: 4g
- Fat: 5g
- Protein: 12g

Turkey, Rabbit and Veal

22.   Turkey Breast

Preparation Time: 12 Hours

Cooking Time: 8 Hours

Servings: 6

Ingredients:

For the Brine:

- 2 pounds turkey breast, deboned
- 2 tbsp. ground black pepper
- ¼ cup salt
- 1 cup brown sugar:
- 4 cups cold water

For the BBQ Rub:

- 2 tbsp. dried onions
- 2 tbsp. garlic powder
- ¼ cup paprika
- 2 tbsp. ground black pepper
- 1 tbsp. salt
- 2 tbsp. brown sugar:
- 2 tbsp. red chili powder
- 1 tbsp. cayenne pepper
- 2 tbsp. Sugar:
- 2 tbsp. ground cumin

Directions:

1. Prepare the brine and for this, take a large bowl, add salt, black pepper, and Sugar: in it, pour in water, and stir until sugar has dissolved.
2. Place turkey breast in it, submerge it completely, and let it soak for a minimum of 12 hours in the refrigerator.

3. Meanwhile, prepare the BBQ rub and for this, take a small bowl, place all of its ingredients in it and then stir until combined, set aside until required.

4. Then remove turkey breast from the brine and season well with the prepared BBQ rub.

5. When ready to cook, switch on the grill, fill the grill hopper with apple-flavored traegers, power the grill on by using the control panel, select 'smoke' on the temperature dial, or set the temperature to 180°F and let it preheat for a minimum of 15 minutes.

6. When the grill has preheated, open the lid, place turkey breast on the grill grate, shut the grill, change the smoking temperature to 225°F, and smoke for 8 hours until the internal temperature reaches 160°F.

7. When done, transfer turkey to a cutting board, let it rest for 10 minutes, then cut it into slices and serve.

Nutrition:

- Calories: 250
- Fat: 5 g
- Carbs: 31 g
- Protein: 18 g

23.   Apple Wood-Smoked Whole Turkey

Preparation Time: 10 minutes **Cooking Time:** 5 hours

Servings: 6

Ingredients:

- 1 (10- to 12-pound) turkey, giblets removed
- Extra-virgin olive oil, for rubbing
- ¼ cup poultry seasoning
- 8 tbsp. (1 stick) unsalted butter, melted
- ½ cup apple juice
- 2 tsp. dried sage
- 2 tsp. dried thyme

Directions:

1. Supply your smoker with a traeger and follow the manufacturer's specific start-up procedure. Preheat, with the lid closed, to 250°F.
2. Rub the turkey with oil and season with the poultry seasoning inside and out, getting under the skin.
3. In a bowl, combine the melted butter, apple juice, sage, and thyme to use for basting.
4. Put the turkey in a roasting pan, place on the grill, close the lid, and grill for 5 to 6 hours, basting every hour until the skin is brown and crispy, or until a meat thermometer inserted in the thickest part of the thigh reads 165°F.
5. Let the turkey meat rest for about 15 to 20 minutes before carving.

Nutrition: Calories: 180 Carbs: 3g Fat: 2g Protein: 39g

24.   Savory-Sweet Turkey Legs

Preparation Time: 10 minutes

Cooking Time: 5 hours

Servings: 4

Ingredients:

- 1 gallon hot water
- 1 cup curing salt (such as Morton Tender Quick)
- ¼ cup packed light brown Sugar:
- 1 tsp. freshly ground black pepper
- 1 tsp. ground cloves
- 1 bay leaf
- 2 tsp. liquid smoke
- 4 turkey legs
- Mandarin Glaze, for serving

Directions:

1. In a huge container with a lid, stir together the water, curing salt, brown sugar, pepper, cloves, bay leaf, and liquid smoke until the salt and Sugar: are dissolved; let come to room temperature.

2. Submerge the turkey legs in the seasoned brine, cover, and refrigerate overnight.

3. When ready to smoke, remove the turkey legs from the brine and rinse them; discard the brine.

4. Supply your smoker with a traeger and follow the manufacturer's specific start-up procedure. Preheat, with the lid closed, to 225°F.

5. Arrange the turkey legs on the grill, close the lid, and smoke for 4 to 5 hours, or until dark brown and a meat thermometer inserted in the thickest part of the meat reads 165°F.

6. Serve with Mandarin Glaze on the side or drizzled over the turkey legs.

Nutrition:

- Calories: 190
- Carbs: 1g
- Fat: 9g
- Protein: 24g

25. Marinated Smoked Turkey Breast

Preparation Time: 15 minutes

Cooking Time: 4 hours

Servings: 6

Ingredients:

- 1 (5 pounds) boneless chicken breast
- 4 cups water
- 2 tbsp. kosher salt
- 1 tsp. Italian seasoning
- 2 tbsp. honey
- 1 tbsp. cider vinegar

Rub:

- ½ tsp. onion powder
- 1 tsp. paprika
- 1 tsp. salt
- 1 tsp. ground black pepper
- 1 tbsp. brown sugar:
- ½ tsp. garlic powder
- 1 tsp. oregano

Directions:

1. In a huge container, combine the water, honey, cider vinegar, Italian seasoning and salt.
2. Add the chicken breast and toss to combine. Cover the bowl and place it in the refrigerator and chill for 4 hours.
3. Rinse the chicken breast with water and pat dry with paper towels.
4. In another mixing bowl, combine the brown sugar, salt, paprika, onion powder, pepper, oregano and garlic.

5. Generously season the chicken breasts with the rub mix.

6. Preheat the grill to 225°F with the lid closed for 15 minutes. Use cherry traegers.

7. Arrange the turkey breast into a grill rack. Place the grill rack on the grill.

8. Smoke for about 3 to 4 hours or until the internal temperature of the turkey breast reaches 165°F.

9. Remove the chicken breast from heat and let them rest for a few minutes. Serve.

Nutrition:

- Calories: 903
- Fat: 34g
- Carbs: 9.9g
- Protein: 131.5g

Game Recipes

26.   Venison Meatloaf

Preparation Time: 20 minutes

Cooking Time: 1 ½ hour

Servings: 5

Ingredients:

- 2 lbs. ground venison
- 1 Diced onion
- 1 Beaten egg
- 1 Pinch salt
- 1 Pinch pepper
- 1 tbsp. Worcestershire sauce
- 1 cup bread crumbs
- 1 oz packet onion soup mix
- 1 cup milk

For the glaze topping

- ¼ cup ketchup
- ¼ cup brown sugar
- ¼ cup apple cider vinegar

Directions:

1. When you are ready to cook, start your Traeger grill on smoke with the lid open for about 4 to 5 minutes
2. Set the temperature to about 350°F and preheat with the lid close for about 10 to 15 minutes

3. Spray a loaf pan with cooking spray; then in a large bowl combine altogether the ground venison with the onion, the egg, the salt, the pepper, and the breadcrumbs

4. Add the Worcestershire sauce, the milk, and the onion soup packet, and be careful not to over mix.

5. In a small bowl, mix the ketchup, brown sugar, and the apple cider vinegar.

6. Spread half of the glaze on the bottom and the sides of the pan; then add the meatloaf and spread the remaining quantity on top of the meatloaf

7. Directly place on the smoker grill grate and smoke for about 1 hour and 15 minutes

8. Let the meatloaf cool for several minutes before slicing it

9. Serve and enjoy your dish!

Nutrition:

- Calories: 219
- Fat: 15g
- Carbs: 0.8g
- Fiber: 0.3g
- Protein: 30g

Burger and Sandwich Recipes

27. Delicious Grilled Chicken Sandwich

Preparation Time: 15 minutes

Cooking Time: 50 minutes

Servings: 4

Ingredients:

- ¼ cup mayonnaise
- 1 tbsp. Dijon mustard
- 1 tbsp. honey
- 4 boneless and skinless chicken breasts
- ½ tsp. steak seasoning
- 4 slices American Swiss cheese
- 4 hamburger buns
- 2 bacon strips
- Lettuce leaves and tomato slices

Directions:

1. Using a small mixing bowl, add in the mayonnaise, mustard, and honey then mix properly to combine.
2. Use a meat mallet to pound the chicken into even thickness then slice into four parts. Season the chicken with the steak seasoning then set aside.
3. Preheat a Traeger Smoker and Grill to 350°F for about ten to fifteen minutes with its lid closed.
4. Place the seasoned chicken on the grill and grill for about twenty-five to thirty minutes until it reads an internal temperature of 165°F. Grill the bacon until crispy then crumble.

5. Add the cheese to the chicken and cook for about one minute until it melts completely. At the same time, grill the buns for about one to two minutes until it is toasted as desired.

6. Place the chicken on the buns, top with the grilled bacon, mayonnaise mixture, lettuce, and tomato then serve.

Nutrition:

- Calories: 410
- Fat: 17g
- Carbohydrate: 29g
- Fiber: 3g

Protein: 34g

Vegetables and Vegetarian Recipes

28. Crispy Garlic Potatoes

Preparation Time: 15 minutes

Cooking Time: 40 minutes

Servings: 4

Ingredients:

- 1 pound baby potatoes, scrubbed
- 1 large white onion, peeled, sliced
- 3 garlic, peeled, sliced
- 1 tsp. chopped parsley
- 3 tbsp. butter, unsalted, sliced

Directions:

1. In the meantime, cut potatoes in slices and then arrange them on a large piece of foil or baking sheet, separating potatoes by onion slices and butter.
2. Sprinkle garlic slices over vegetables, and then season with salt, black pepper, and parsley.
3. When the grill has preheated, place a baking sheet containing potato mixture on the grilling rack and grill for 40 minutes until potato slices have turned tender.
4. Serve immediately.

Nutrition:

- Calories: 150
- Carbs: 15g
- Fat: 10g
- Protein: 1g

29.   Stuffed Avocados

Preparation Time: 5 minutes

Cooking Time: 10 to 15 minutes

Servings: 3 to 4

Ingredients:

- 4 Avocados, Halved, Pit Removed
- 8 Eggs
- 2 cups Shredded Cheddar Cheese
- 4 Slices Bacon, Cooked and Chopped
- ¼ cup Cherry Tomatoes, Halved
- Green Onions, Sliced Thin
- Salt and Pepper, To Taste

Directions:

1. When ready to cook, set the temperature to High and preheat, lid closed for 15 minutes.
2. After removing the pit from the avocado, scoop out a little of the flesh to make enough room to fit 1 egg per half.
3. Fill the bottom of a cast Iron: pan with kosher salt and nestle the avocado halves into the salt, cut side up. The salt helps to keep them in place while cooking, like ice with oysters.
4. Crack an egg into each half, top with a hand full of shredded cheddar cheese, some cherry tomatoes, and bacon. Season with salt and pepper to taste.

5. Place the cast Iron: pan directly on the grill grate and bake the avocados for 12-15 minutes until the cheese is melted and the egg is just set.

6. Remove from the grill and let rest 5-10 minutes. Enjoy!

Nutrition:

- Carbs: 50g
- Fat: 103g
- Protein: 58g

30.   Bacon-Wrapped Asparagus

Preparation Time: 10 minutes

Cooking Time: 25 to 30 minutes

Servings: 3

Ingredients:

- 1-pound fresh thick asparagus (15 to 20 spears)
- extra-virgin olive oil
- 5 slices thinly sliced bacon
- 1 tsp. Pete's Western Rub or salt and pepper

Directions:

1. Snap off the woody ends of asparagus and trim so they are all about the same length.
2. Divide the asparagus into bundles of 3 spears and spritz with olive oil. Wrap each bundle with 1 piece of bacon and then dust with the seasoning or salt and pepper to taste.
3. Configure your Traeger smoker-grill for indirect cooking, placing Teflon coated fiberglass mats on top of the grates (to prevent the asparagus from sticking to the grill grates). Preheat to 400°F using any type of Traegers. The grill can be preheated while prepping the asparagus.
4. Grill the bacon-wrapped asparagus for 25 to 30 minutes, until the asparagus is tender and the bacon is cooked and crispy.

Nutrition: Calories: 94 Carbs: 5g Fat: 7g Protein: 4g

31.Brisket Baked Beans

Preparation Time: 15 minutes

Cooking Time: 1 to 2 hours

Servings: 5

Ingredients:

- 2 tbsp. extra-virgin olive oil 1 large yellow onion, diced
- 1 medium green bell pepper, diced
- 1 medium red bell pepper, diced
- 2 to 6 jalapeño peppers, diced
- 3 cups chopped Texas-Style Brisket Flat (page 91) 1 (28-ounce) can baked beans, like Bush's Country
- Style Baked Beans 1 (28-ounce) can pork and beans
- 1 (14-ounce) can red kidney beans, rinsed and drained 1 cup barbecue sauce, like Sweet Baby Ray's
- Barbecue Sauce ½ cup packed brown sugar
- 3 garlic cloves, chopped
- 2 tsp. ground mustard
- ½ tsp. kosher salt
- ½ tsp. black pepper

Directions:

1. In a skillet over medium heat, warm the olive oil and then add the diced onion, peppers, and jalapeños. Cook until the onions are translucent, about 8 to 10 minutes, stirring occasionally.

2. In a 4-quart casserole dish, mix the chopped brisket, baked beans, pork and beans, kidney beans, cooked onion and

peppers, barbecue sauce, brown sugar, garlic, ground mustard, salt, and black pepper.

3. Configure your Traeger smoker-grill for indirect cooking and preheat to 325°F using your Traegers of choice. Cook the brisket baked beans uncovered for 1½ to 2 hours until the beans are thick and bubbly. Allow resting for 15 minutes before serving.

Nutrition:

- Carbs: 35g
- Fat: 2g
- Protein: 9g

32.   Garlic Parmesan Wedges

Preparation Time: 15 minutes

Cooking Time: 45 minutes

Servings: 6

Ingredients:

- 3 large russet potatoes
- ¼ cup extra-virgin olive oil
- 1½ tsp. salt
- ¾ tsp. black pepper
- 2 tsp. garlic powder
- ¾ cup grated Parmesan cheese
- 3 tbsp. chopped fresh cilantro or flat-leaf parsley (optional)
- ½ cup blue cheese or ranch dressing per serving, for dipping (optional)

Directions:

1. Gently scrub the potatoes with cold water using a vegetable brush and allow the potatoes to dry.
2. Cut the potatoes lengthwise in half, and then cut those halves into thirds.
3. Use a paper towel to wipe away all the moisture that is released when you cut the potatoes. Moisture prevents the wedges from getting crispy.
4. Place the potato wedges, olive oil, salt, pepper, and garlic powder in a large bowl, and toss lightly with your hands, making sure the oil and spices are distributed evenly.

5. Arrange the wedges in a single layer on a nonstick grilling tray/pan/basket (about 15 × 12 inches).

6. Configure your Traeger smoker-grill for indirect cooking and preheat to 425°F using any type of Traegers.

7. Place the grilling tray in your preheated smoker-grill and roast the potato wedges for 15 minutes before turning. Roast the potato wedges for an additional 15 to 20 minutes until potatoes are fork-tender on the inside and crispy golden brown on the outside.

8. Sprinkle the potato wedges with Parmesan cheese and garnish with cilantro or parsley, if desired. Serve with blue cheese or ranch dressing for dipping, if desired.

Nutrition:

- Calories: 324
- Fat: 11.6g
- Cholesterol: 6mg
- Protein: 8.6g

Fish & Seafood Recipes

33.   Smoked Shrimp

Preparation Time: 4 hours and 15 minutes

Cooking Time: 10 minutes

Servings: 4

Ingredients:

- 4 tbsp. olive oil
- 1 tbsp. Cajun seasoning
- 2 cloves garlic, minced
- 1 tbsp. lemon juice
- Salt to taste
- 2 lb. shrimp, peeled and deveined

Direction:

1. Combine all the ingredients in a sealable plastic bag.
2. Toss to coat evenly.
3. Marinate in the refrigerator for 4 hours.
4. Set the Traeger grill to high.
5. Preheat it for 15 minutes while the lid is closed.
6. Thread shrimp onto skewers.
7. Grill for 4 minutes per side.

Serving suggestion: Garnish with lemon wedges.

Preparation/Cooking Tips: Soak skewers first in water if you are using wooden skewers.

Nutrition: Calories: 298 Protein: 42g Carbs: 10g Fat: 10g Fiber: 0g

34.   Cod with Lemon Herb Butter

Preparation Time: 30 minutes Cooking Time: 15 minutes

Servings: 4

Ingredients:

- 4 tbsp. butter
- 1 clove garlic, minced
- 1 tbsp. tarragon, chopped
- 1 tbsp. lemon juice
- 1 tsp. lemon zest
- Salt and pepper to taste
- 1 lb. cod fillet

Direction:

1. Preheat the Traeger grill to high heat for 15 minutes while the lid is closed.
2. In a bowl, mix the butter, garlic, tarragon, lemon juice and lemon zest, salt, and pepper.
3. Place the fish in a baking pan.
4. Spread the butter mixture on top.
5. Bake the fish for 15 minutes.

Serving suggestion: Spoon sauce over the fish before serving.

Preparation/Cooking Tips: You can also use other white fish fillets for this recipe.

Nutrition: Calories: 218 Protein: 22g Carbs: 20g Fat: 12g   Fiber: 0g

35. Salmon with Avocado Salsa

Preparation Time: 30 minutes Cooking Time: 20 minutes

Servings: 6 Ingredients:

- 3 lb. salmon fillet
- Garlic salt and pepper to taste
- 4 cups avocado, sliced into cubes
- 1 onion, chopped
- 1 jalapeño pepper, minced
- 1 tbsp. lime juice
- 1 tbsp. olive oil
- ¼ cup cilantro, chopped
- Salt to taste

Direction:

1. Sprinkle both sides of salmon with garlic salt and pepper.
2. Set the Traeger grill to smoke.
3. Grill the salmon for 7 to 8 minutes per side.
4. While waiting, prepare the salsa by combining the remaining ingredients in a bowl.
5. Serve salmon with the avocado salsa.

Serving suggestion: Garnish with lemon wedges.

Preparation/Cooking Tips: You can also use tomato salsa for this recipe if you don't have avocados.

Nutrition: Calories: 278 Protein: 20g Carbs: 17g Fat: 11g Fiber: 0g

36.   Buttered Crab Legs

Preparation Time: 30 minutes

Cooking Time: 10 minutes

Servings: 4

Ingredients:

- 12 tbsp. butter
- 1 tbsp. parsley, chopped
- 1 tbsp. tarragon, chopped
- 1 tbsp. chives, chopped
- 1 tbsp. lemon juice
- 4 lb. king crab legs, split in the center

Direction:

1. Set the Traeger grill to 375°F.
2. Preheat it for 15 minutes while the lid is closed.
3. In a pan over medium heat, simmer the butter, herbs, and lemon juice for 2 minutes.
4. Place the crab legs on the grill.
5. Pour half of the sauce on top.
6. Grill for 10 minutes.
7. Serve with the reserved butter sauce.

Serving suggestion: Garnish with lemon wedges.

Preparation/Cooking Tips: You can also use shrimp for this recipe.

Nutrition: Calories: 218 Protein: 28g Carbs: 18g Fat: 10g Fiber: 0g

37. Grilled Blackened Salmon

Preparation Time: 15 minutes

Cooking Time: 30 minutes

Servings: 4

Ingredients:

- 4 salmon fillet
- Blackened dry rub
- Italian seasoning powder

Direction:

1. Season salmon fillets with the dry rub and seasoning powder.
2. Grill in the Traeger grill at 325°F for 10 to 15 minutes per side.

Serving suggestion: Garnish with lemon wedges.

Preparation/Cooking Tips: You can also drizzle salmon with lemon juice

Nutrition:

- Calories: 258
- Protein: 23g
- Carbs: 20g
- Fat: 12g
- Fiber: 0g

Rub and Sauces Recipes

38.   Smoked Cranberry Sauce

Preparation Time: 10 minutes **Cooking Time:** 1 hour

Servings: 2 Ingredients:

- 12 oz. bag cranberries
- 2 chunks ginger, quartered
- 1 cup apple cider
- 1 tbsp. honey whiskey
- oz. fruit juice
- 1/8 tbsp. ground cloves
- 1/8 tbsp. cinnamon
- ½ orange zest
- ½ orange
- 1 tbsp. maple syrup
- 1 apple, diced and peeled
- ½ cup sugar
- ½ brown sugar

Directions:

1. Preheat your Traeger grill to 375°F.
2. Place cranberries in a pan then add all other ingredients.
3. Place the pan on the grill and cook for about 1 hour until cooked through.
4. Remove ginger pieces and squeeze juices from the orange into the sauce.

Nutrition: Calories: 48 Fat: 0.1g Carbs: 12.3g Protein: 0.4g Fiber: 2.3g

Cheese and Breads

39.   Smoked Cheddar Cheese

Preparation Time: 5 minutes

Cooking Time: 5 hour

Servings: 2

Ingredients:

- 2, 8-oz, cheddar cheese blocks

Directions:

1. Preheat and set your Traeger grill to 90°F.
2. Place the cheese blocks directly on the grill grate and smoke for about 4 hours.
3. Remove and transfer into a plastic bag, resealable. Refrigerate for about 2 weeks to allow flavor from smoke to permeate your cheese.
4. Now enjoy!

Nutrition:

- Calories: 115 Fat: 9.5g
- Saturated Fat: 5.4g
- Carbs: 0.9g
- Net Carbs: 0.9g
- Protein: 6.5g
- Sugars: 0.1g
- Fiber: 0g
- Sodium: 185mg

Potassium: 79mg

Nut, Fruits and Dessert

40.   Traeger Grill Chocolate Chip Cookies

Preparation Time: 20 min

Cooking Time: 45 min

Servings: 12

Ingredients:

- 1cup salted butter, softened
- 1cup sugar
- 1cup light brown sugar
- 2tsp. vanilla extract
- 2large eggs
- 3cups all-purpose flour
- 1tsp. baking soda
- ½ tsp. baking powder
- 1tsp. natural sea salt
- 2cups semi-sweet chocolate chips, or chunks

Directions:

1. Preheat Traeger grill to 375°F.
2. Line a large baking sheet with parchment paper and set aside.
3. In a medium bowl, mix flour, baking soda, salt, and baking powder. Once combined, set aside.
4. In a stand mixer bowl, combine butter, white sugar, and brown sugar until combined. Beat in eggs and vanilla. Beat until fluffy.
5. Mix in dry ingredients, continue to stir until combined.

6. Add chocolate chips and mix thoroughly.

7. Roll 3 tbsp. of dough at a time into balls and place them on your cookie sheet. Evenly space them apart, with about 2-3 inches in between each ball.

8. Place cookie sheet directly on the grill grate and bake for 20-25 minutes, until the outside of the cookies is slightly browned.

9. Remove from grill and allow resting for 10 minutes. Serve and enjoy!

Nutrition:

- Calories: 120
- Fat: 4
- Cholesterol: 7.8 mg
- Carbohydrate: 22.8 g
- Fiber: 0.3 g
- Sugar: 14.4 g
- Protein: 1.4 g

41.Delicious Donuts on a Grill

Preparation Time: 5 minutes

Cooking Time: 10 Minutes

Servings: 6

Ingredients:

- 1-½ cups sugar, powdered
- 1/3 cup whole milk
- ½ tsp. vanilla extract
- 16 ounces biscuit dough, prepared
- Oil spray, for greasing
- 1cup chocolate sprinkles, for sprinkling

Directions:

1. Take a medium bowl and mix sugar, milk, and vanilla extract.
2. Combine well to create a glaze.
3. Set the glaze aside for further use.
4. Place the dough onto the flat, clean surface.
5. Flat the dough with a rolling pin.
6. Use a ring mold, about an inch, and cut a hole in the center of each round dough.
7. Place the dough on a plate and refrigerate for 10 minutes.
8. Open the grill and install the grill grate inside it.
9. Close the hood.
10. Now, select the grill from the menu, and set the temperature to medium.

11. Set the time to 6 minutes.

12. Select start and begin preheating.

13. Remove the dough from the refrigerator and coat it with cooking spray from both sides.

14. When the unit beeps, the grill is preheated; place the adjustable amount of dough on the grill grate.

15. Close the hood, and cook for 3 minutes.

16. After 3 minutes, remove donuts and place the remaining dough inside.

17. Cook for 3 minutes.

18. Once all the donuts are ready, sprinkle chocolate sprinkles on top.

19. Enjoy.

Nutrition:

- Calories: 400
- Fat: 11g
- Saturated Fat: 4.2g
- Cholesterol: 1mg
- Sodium: 787mg
- Carbs: 71.3g
- Fiber: 0.9g
- Sugars: 45.3g
- Protein: 5.7g

Lamb Recipes

42.   Pistachio Roasted Lamb

Preparation Time: 20 minutes

Cooking Time: 40 minutes

Servings: 6

Ingredients:

Traegers:

- 1 tbsp. vegetable oil
- 2 lamb racks
- 3 carrots, peeled and chopped
- 1 lb. potatoes
- 1 tbsp. olive oil
- ½ tsp. salt
- ½ tsp. pepper
- 1 clove garlic, minced
- 2 tsp. thyme
- 3 cups pistachios
- 2 tbsp. breadcrumbs
- 1 tbsp. butter
- 1 tsp. olive oil
- 3 tbsp. Dijon mustard

Directions:

1. When ready to cook, set your smoker to 450°F and preheat.
2. Place a large pan on the grill and add vegetable oil.
3. Pat the lamb dry and then season each rack of lamb with salt and black pepper.

4. Add the carrots to a mixing bowl with the salt, potatoes, garlic, olive oil, pepper, and thyme. Set aside.

5. Place lamb in the pan and cook for eight minutes. Transfer lamb from the grill to rest before mixing the pistachios, butter, salt, bread crumbs, and olive oil

6. Spread mustard on the fat-side of each rack of lamb. Pat pistachio mixture on top of the mustard.

7. Place the carrots and lamb onto the pan and then cook them alongside the lamb for 15 minutes.

8. Open the lid and cook for ten more minutes before serving.

Nutrition:

- Calories: 50
- Carbs: 4g
- Fiber: 2g
- Fat: 2.5g
- Protein: 2g

43.   Lamb Wraps

Preparation Time: 1 hour

Cooking Time: 2 hours

Servings: 4

Ingredients:

Traegers: Apple

- 1 leg lamb
- 3 lemons, juiced
- Olive oil
- Big game rub
- 2 cups yogurt
- 2 cucumbers, diced
- 2 cloves garlic, minced
- 4 tbsp. dill, finely diced
- 2 tbsp. mint leaves, finely diced
- Salt and pepper
- 12 pitas
- 3 tomatoes, diced
- 1 red onion, thinly sliced
- 8 oz. feta cheese

Directions:

1. Rub your lamb with lemon juice, olive oil, and rub.
2. When ready to cook, set your smoker temperature to 500°F and preheat. Put the leg of lamb on the smoker and cook for 30 minutes.

3. Lower the heat to 350°F and keep cooking for another hour.

4. While the lamb is roasting, create the tzatziki sauce by mixing the yogurt, cucumbers, garlic, dill, mint leaves, in a bowl and mix to combine. Place in the refrigerator to chill.

5. Get the pittas and wrap them in foil, then place them on the grill to warm.

6. Put the lamb on a cutting board and leave to rest for 15 minutes before slicing.

7. Fill the warm pita with red onion, lamb, diced tomato, tzatziki sauce, and feta.

Nutrition:

- Calories: 50
- Carbs: 4g
- Fiber: 2g
- Fat: 2.5g
- Protein: 2g

44.   Moroccan Kebabs

Preparation Time: 20 minutes

Cooking Time: 30 minutes

Servings: 2

Ingredients:

Traegers: Cherry

- 1 cup onions, finely diced
- 1 tbsp. fresh mint, finely diced
- 1 tsp. paprika
- 1 tsp. salt
- ½ tsp. ground coriander
- ¼ tsp. ground cinnamon
- Pita Bread
- 2 cloves garlic, minced
- 3 tbsp. cilantro leaves, finely diced
- 1 tbsp. ground cumin
- 1 ½ lb. ground lamb

Directions:

1. In a bowl, mix the ingredients except for the pita bread. Mix into meatballs, and skewer each meatball.
2. Next, wet your hands with water and shape the meat into a sausage shape about as large as your thumb. Cover and refrigerate for 30 minutes.

3. When ready to cook, set your smoker temperature to 350°F and preheat. Put the kebabs on the smoker and cook for 30 minutes.

4. Serve with the pita bread.

Nutrition:

- Calories: 316
- Carbs: 19g
- Protein: 26g
- Fat: 29g

Appetizers and Sides

45.   Smashed Potato Casserole

Preparation Time: 30-45 minutes

Cooking Time: 45-60 minutes

Servings: 8

Recommended Traeger: Optional

Ingredients:

- 8-10 bacon slices
- ¼ cup (½ stick) salt butter or bacon grease
- 1 sliced red onion
- 1 sliced small pepper
- 1 sliced small red pepper
- 1 sliced small pepper
- 3 cups mashed potatoes
- ¾ cup sour cream
- 1.5 tsp. Texas BBQ Love
- 3 cups sharp cheddar cheese
- 4 cups hashed brown potato

Directions:

1. Cook the bacon in a large skillet over medium heat until both sides are crispy for about 5 minutes. Set the bacon aside.
2. Transfer the rendered bacon grease to a glass container.
3. In the same large frying pan, heat the butter or bacon grease over medium heat and fry the red onions and peppers until they become al dente. Set aside.

4. Spray a 9 x 11-inch casserole dish with a non-stick cooking spray and spread the mashed potatoes to the bottom of the dish.

5. Layer sour cream on mashed potatoes and season with Texas BBQ Love.

6. Layer the stir-fried vegetables on the potatoes and pour butter or bacon grease into a pan.

7. Sprinkle 1.5 cups of sharp cheddar cheese followed by frozen hash brown potatoes.

8. Spoon the remaining butter or bacon grease from the stir-fried vegetables over the hash browns and place the crushed bacon.

9. Place the remaining 1.5 cups of sharp cheddar cheese and cover the casserole dish with a lid or aluminum foil.

10. Set up a Traeger smoking grill for indirect cooking and preheat to 350°F.

11. Bake the crushed potato casserole for 45-60 minutes until the cheese foams.

12. Rest for 10 minutes before eating.

Nutrition:

- Calories: 330
- Carbs: 13g
- Protein: 11g
- Fat: 20g

46.   Mushrooms Stuffed with Crab Meat

Preparation Time: 20 minutes

Cooking Time: 30-45 minutes

Servings: 4-6

Recommended Traeger: Optional

Ingredients:

- 6 medium-sized Portobello mushrooms
- Extra virgin olive oil
- 1/3 Grated parmesan cheese cup
- Club Beat Staffing:
- 8 oz. fresh crab meat or canned or imitation crab meat
- 2 tbsp. extra virgin olive oil
- 1/3 Chopped celery
- Chopped red peppers
- ½ cup chopped green onion
- ½ cup Italian breadcrumbs
- ½cup mayonnaise
- 8 oz. cream cheese at room temperature
- ½ tsp. garlic
- 1 tbsp. dried parsley
- Grated parmesan cheese cup
- 1 1 tsp. Old Bay seasoning
- ¼ tsp. kosher salt
- ¼ tsp. black pepper

Directions:

1. Clean the mushroom cap with a damp paper towel. Cut off the stem and save it.
2. Remove the brown gills from the bottom of the mushroom cap with a spoon and discard.
3. Prepare crab meat stuffing. If you are using canned crab meat, drain, rinse, and remove shellfish.
4. Heat the olive oil in a frying pan over medium-high heat. Add celery, peppers, and green onions and fry for 5 minutes. Set aside for cooling.
5. Gently pour the chilled sautéed vegetables and the remaining ingredients into a large bowl.
6. Cover and refrigerate crab meat stuffing until ready to use.
7. Put the crab mixture in each mushroom cap and make a mound in the center.
8. Sprinkle extra virgin olive oil and sprinkle parmesan cheese on each stuffed mushroom cap. Put the mushrooms in a 10 x 15-inch baking dish.
9. Set the Traeger smoker grill to indirect heating and preheat to 375°F.
10. Bake for 30-45 minutes until the filling becomes hot (165°F as measured by an instant-read digital thermometer) and the mushrooms begin to release juice.

Nutrition:

- Calories: 456
- Carbs: 14g
- Protein: 29g
- Fat: 17g

47.   Bacon Wrapped with Asparagus

Preparation Time: 15 minutes

Cooking Time: 25-30 minutes

Servings: 4-6

Recommended Traeger: Optional

- 1-pound fresh thick asparagus (15-20 spears)
- Extra virgin olive oil
- 5 slices bacon
- 1 tsp. Western Love or salted pepper

Directions:

1. Cut off the wooden ends of the asparagus and make them all the same length.
2. Divide the asparagus into a bundle of three spears and split with olive oil. Wrap each bundle with a piece of bacon, then dust with seasonings or salt pepper for seasoning.
3. Set the Traeger smoker grill for indirect cooking and place a Teflon coated fiberglass mat on the grate (to prevent asparagus from sticking to the grate). Preheat to 400°F using all types of Traegers. The grill can be preheated during the asparagus Preparation Guide.
4. Bake the asparagus wrapped in bacon for 25-30 minutes until the asparagus is soft and the bacon is cooked and crispy.

Nutrition: Calories: 321 Carbs: 18g Protein: 27g Fat: 23g

48.   Onion Bacon Ring

Preparation Time: 10 Minutes

Cooking Time: 1 Hour and 30 Minutes

Servings: 6 to 8

Ingredients:

- 2 large Onions, cut into ½ inch slices
- 1 Package Bacon
- 1 tsp. Honey
- 1 tbsp. Mustard, yellow
- 1 tbsp. Garlic chili sauce

Direction:

1. Wrap Bacon around onion rings. Wrap until you out of bacon. Place on skewers.
2. Preheat the grill to 400°F with a closed lid.
3. In the meantime, in a bowl combine the mustard and garlic chili sauce. Add honey and stir well.
4. Grill the onion bacon rings for 1 h and 30 minutes. Flip once.
5. Serve with the sauce and enjoy!

Nutrition:

- Calories: 90
- Protein: 2g
- Carbs: 9g
- Fat: 7g

Traditional Recipes

49.　Halibut Delight

Preparation Time: 4-6 hours

Cooking Time: 15 minutes

Servings: 4-6

Ingredients:

- ½ a cup of salt

- ½ a cup of brown Sugar:

- 1 tsp. of smoked paprika

- 1 tsp. of ground cumin

- 2 pound of halibut

- 1/3 cup of mayonnaise

Directions:

1. Take a small bowl and add salt, brown Sugar:, cumin, and paprika

2. Coat the halibut well and cover, refrigerate for 4-6 hours

3. Take your drip pan and add water, cover with aluminum foil. Pre-heat your smoker to 200°F

4. Use water fill water pan halfway through and place it over drip pan. Add wood chips to the side tray

5. Remove the fish from refrigerator and rinse it well, pat it dry

6. Rub the mayonnaise on the fish

7. Transfer the halibut to smoker and smoke for 2 hours until the internal temperature reaches 120°Fahrenheit

Nutrition:

- Calories: 375

- Fats: 21g

- Carbs: 10g

- Fiber: 2g

50. Roast Rack of Lamb

Preparation Time: 10 minutes

Cooking Time: 1 hour

Servings: 6-8

Ingredients:

- Traeger Flavor: Alder

- 1 (2-pound) rack of lamb

- 1 batch Rosemary-Garlic Lamb Seasoning

Directions:

1. Supply your smoker with traegers and follow the manufacturer's specific start-up procedure. Preheat the grill to 450°F.

2. Using a boning knife, score the bottom fat portion of the rib meat.

3. Using your hands, rub the rack of lamb with the lamb seasoning, making sure it penetrates into the scored fat.

4. Place the rack directly on the grill grate and smoke until its internal temperature reaches 145F.

5. Take off the rack from the grill and let it rest for 20 to 30 minutes, before slicing into individual ribs to serve.

Nutrition: Calories: 50 Carbs: 4g Fiber: 2g Fat: 2.5g Protein: 2g

Conclusion

Traeger grills are revolutionary and may forever change the way we cook.

These days, anyone can own a Traeger grill since manufacturers meet the demand of clients from various backgrounds.

Modern Traeger grills make cooking enjoyable and hassle-free.

It also eliminates guesswork thanks to the easy-to-follow recipes and the ability to remotely monitor and adjust your temperatures.

Whether you're an amateur home cook hosting a backyard cookout or a pitmaster at a barbecue competition, a Traeger grill can easily become one of the most important appliances you can own to help you make flavorful meals with much less effort.

Although Traegers grill isn't everyone's favorite choice, it's clear that it is a must-have outdoor kitchen appliance. Whether you love smoking, grilling, roasting, barbecuing, or direct cooking of food, the Traeger grill is clearly versatile and has got you covered.

Cooking with a Traeger grill allows you to choose the desired flavor of Traegers to create the perfect smoke to flavor your food. Each Traeger type has its personality and taste. The best part is you can use a single flavor or experiment with mixing and matching the flavors to invent your own combination.

Just like any cooking appliance, Traegers have some drawbacks but the benefits overshadow them. It is therefore definitely worth a try.

These days, one popular method of cooking is smoking, which many enthusiasts use. Proteins such as different kinds of meat, poultry, and fish would be ruined quickly if modern techniques in cooking are used. Smoking, on the other hand, is a process that takes a long time and low temperature, which thoroughly cooks the meat. The smoke, especially white smoke, greatly enhances the flavor of almost any food item. But more than that, smoking seals and preserves the nutrients in the food. Smoking is flexible and is one of the oldest techniques for making food.

The picture of a good time with loved ones, neighbors, and friends having a backyard barbeque is a pretty sight, isn't it? Having a smoker-grill and some grilled and smoked recipes are excellent when you have visitors at home because you can deliver both tasty food and a magical moment on a summer night, for example. Hundreds of awesome recipes are available that you can try with a Traeger smoker-grill! Experiment, improve, or make your own recipes – it is up to you. You can do it fast and easy. But if you want to be safe with the proven and tested ones, by all means, do so. These recipes have been known to be just right to the taste and they work every time. A combination of creating a correct impression the first time and every time and enjoying scrumptious food along the way will be your edge.

Another great thing about these recipes is that they are easy to prepare and do not require you to be a wizard in the kitchen. Simply by following a few easy steps and having the right ingredients at your disposal, you can use these recipes to make some delicious food in no time. So, try these recipes and spread the word! I'm sure this Traeger smoker-grill recipe book will prove to be an invaluable gift to your loved ones, too!

Finally, while you will have fantastic smoking and grilling time with whichever Traeger grill model you choose, the models are quite different. They offer different services and are suitable for different users. With the new Traeger grill series being produced each year, you need to shop smartly so that you buy a grill that perfectly fits you and meets all your needs.

If you are considering buying a grill yourself, then first you need to know is the best kind of grills out in the market and what will suit you. You need to know how they work, and compare which ones are trending. Traeger Grill is top on the markets and has many advantages over the standard cooking grill everyone has. New technology is coming out with better and better products to choose from, and if you don't upgrade your purchase and keep buying the same old stuff, then you will be left behind.

The Traeger grill provides a person which a great barbecuing experience with everyone, making food tastes better and cooking easier.

CPSIA information can be obtained
at www.ICGtesting.com
Printed in the USA
LVHW020822050521
686547LV00006B/433